Monsters
and Mythical Creatures

Goblins

Other titles in the Monsters and Mythical Creatures series include:

Aliens
Cyclops
Demons
Dragons
Water Monsters
Zombies

Monsters
and Mythical Creatures

Goblins

Stephen Currie

ReferencePoint
Press®

San Diego, CA

LIBRARY OF CONGRESS CATALOGING-IN-PUBLICATION DATA

Currie, Stephen, 1960–
  Goblins / by Stephen Currie.
    p. cm. — (Monsters and mythical creatures)
  Includes bibliographical references and index.
  ISBN-13: 978-1-60152-149-1 (hardback)
  ISBN-10: 1-60152-149-9 (hardback)
  1. Goblins. I. Title.
  GR549.C87 2011
  398.24'54—dc22
                                                    2010038863

Contents

Goblins in Legends and Literature

A man clutching his young son is riding a horse through a dark forest at night. A strong wind is blowing, and fog is floating among the trees. The forest is spooky, and the little boy is scared of what might be lurking in the woods. He is particularly afraid of a bloodthirsty creature known as the Erlking, a supernatural being believed to attack travelers who pass through the forest. As the horse hurries along the trail, the boy seems to see something just off the path—a living thing that tries to talk to him. "Father, the Erlking! Can you not see?" he asks anxiously. "The dreadful Erlking with crown and tail?"[1]

The father, however, notices nothing strange. He assures his son that he has no reason to worry. What the boy thinks is the Erlking is just a wisp of fog, he says. As for the voice the boy says he heard, the father tells him it is only the

> ## Did You Know?
>
> The story of the Erlking goblin was set to music by German composer Franz Schubert in 1815. Schubert's music for the poem is a famous example of how composers use dramatic tension when setting poems to music.

whistling of the wind. But he is wrong: The Erlking *is* lurking in the woods, and the creature suddenly jumps out to attack the boy. Alarmed, the father urges the horse to go faster. When the pair reach home, though, he discovers that the boy has died in his arms—killed by the Erlking.

The Erlking is part of the folklore of Germany, and the story of the man and his son comes from a poem by a German writer named Johann Wilhelm von Goethe. Different stories describe the Erlking in different ways. Most sources agree, though, that the Erlking is strong, small, and vicious, and that little can be done to fight it

Mythical creatures such as dwarves, elves, dragons, and goblins (pictured here in a scene from the 2002 film The Lord of the Rings: The Two Towers *) fill the pages of J.R.R. Tolkien's classic stories. Goblins also appear in many folktales.*

off. The Erlking is one of many similar creatures appearing in folk stories, novels, and poetry all over the world—creatures known to us as goblins.

Goblins in Literature

Goblins appear in the folklore of many lands and cultures. They seem particularly common in tales from two parts of the world. One is northern Europe, notably Germany, Scandinavia, and the British Isles. The other is eastern Asia, especially Japan. Still, goblins can easily be found in the folktales of other places as well. Indeed, goblins are important characters in traditional stories in places ranging from India to Italy and from Russia to the Middle East.

Goblins are featured in stories besides folktales, too. In the 1800s and early 1900s, some fiction writers used themes and characters from folklore in their original work. Many of the resulting novels and short stories deal with legendary creatures, often including goblins. The best known of these works today are J.R.R. Tolkien's classic fantasies *The Hobbit* and *The Lord of the Rings* trilogy; each is built around mythical characters such as dwarves, elves, and dragons, and goblins are an important part of the storylines as well. Some books of the period even use goblins as main characters. In 1871 for instance, British writer George MacDonald published a fantasy novel called *The Princess and the Goblin*.

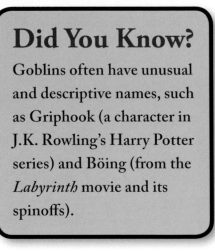

Did You Know?

Goblins often have unusual and descriptive names, such as Griphook (a character in J.K. Rowling's Harry Potter series) and Böing (from the *Labyrinth* movie and its spinoffs).

In recent years, interest in fantasy fiction has grown rapidly. Many creative people have followed in the footsteps of writers like Tolkien and MacDonald by dreaming up mythical worlds where strange and sometimes dangerous characters live. Some of these people are novelists who write books for adults, while some write stories aimed primarily at young people. Still others work in newer media, such as role-playing games and film.

Information about goblins, then, can come from any of these sources. In truth, though, the exact source of a goblin story is less important than the story itself. Tales about monsters and mythical beasts have always appealed to readers and listeners. People are drawn to stories that involve danger and the unknown, and narratives about legendary creatures such as the Erlking offer both. Whether the goblins in the stories are murderous or simply annoying, whether they destroy their human enemies or are outwitted by the people they struggle against, tales of goblins have entertained generations of listeners and readers. In all likelihood, they will continue to do so for many generations to come.

Chapter 1

A Field Guide to Goblins

Many creatures of myth and legend are easy to identify. The Loch Ness monster, which is said to inhabit a deep lake in Scotland, is an excellent example. Every story about the Loch Ness monster describes it more or less the same way: as an enormous snakelike creature whose body surges up and down as it swims. Another example is Bigfoot, a creature believed by some to live in the forests of the Pacific Northwest. Nearly all sources agree that Bigfoot has dark fur, resembles an ape, and walks on two legs. The same is true of werewolves, giants, and many other mythical monsters. The descriptions of these creatures are consistent from one source to the next, and a person who sees one of these creatures will usually recognize it right away.

That is not the case for goblins. The descriptions of goblins vary considerably from one culture to the next and from one story to another. Goblins make their homes in caves, or in the walls of human houses, or in cracks below the ground; their ears are red, or green, or multicolored; they run in packs, or they live in small family units. Because goblins have no standard description, they are often confused with similar-sized legendary creatures such as elves and brownies. Indeed, in some ways the term *goblin* simply refers to any smallish, unpleasant creature that is not obviously something else.

Small, Ugly, and Quarrelsome

Although a goblin cannot be easily recognized just by looking at it, the majority of goblins do share certain characteristics. One of these is size. While a few goblins are tall—one appearing in J.R.R. Tolkien's classic novel *The Fellowship of the Ring* is described as "almost man-high"[2]—most goblins are short. The Italian folktale "The Three Silver Balls," for example, tells of a goblin that is about the same height as a human child. An Estonian story called "The Cook and the House Goblin" is about an even smaller goblin, one tiny enough to make its home under an oven. And in Megan McDonald's picture book *Hinky Pink*, the goblin is scarcely any larger than a flea. Most goblins seem to measure somewhere between the height of an adult male's knee and chest.

Similarly, nearly all sources agree that goblins are unattractive, even grotesque. "Out jumped the goblins," writes Tolkien in *The Hobbit*, "great ugly-looking goblins, lots of goblins."[3] According to the Spiderwick Chronicles, a fantasy series by Tony DiTerlizzi and Holly Black, goblins have unsightly growths all over their bodies. And a traditional folktale called "The Goblins at the Bath House" has a character that is described as "a hideous little goblin man with glaring eyes and bandy legs."[4]

A third feature common to most goblins is temperament. The majority of goblins are quarrelsome and self-centered—and descriptions of their unpleasantness are found in many stories, whether modern fantasy tales or traditional folk stories. Early in J.T. Petty's fantasy novel *Clemency Pogue: The Hobgoblin Proxy*, for instance, one character tells another, "Goblins are nothing but chaos and nastiness [and] toe-jam sandwiches."[5]

Even in stories where no one states that goblins are disagreeable, the reader soon figures it out. In one traditional European story, for example, a young man comes upon three goblins in a

forest. The goblins are busily fighting one another; according to one retelling of the story, they were "thumping each other on their little backs, biting, kicking, tearing each other's hair, and screaming."[6] In some stories, the goblins' unpleasantness goes even further. An Asian folktale introduces a group of goblins by describing the sudden fury of the leader when his dogs will not stop barking. "Kill those worthless beasts!"[7] he orders, and an underling quickly carries out the command.

A final similarity shared by goblins is age. Nearly all sources agree that goblins live much longer than humans. A guide to the strange creatures in the Spiderwick series has a full-color portrait of what the authors identify as a Greater Bull Goblin. According to a note in the text, the goblin was drawn from life, and the model was 147 years old at the time the picture was made. In George MacDonald's *The Princess and the Goblin*, a father goblin points out that his son still has much to learn. The implication is that the younger goblin is still a boy. Measured in human terms, however, that is not the case. "You were only fifty last month,"[8] the father explains.

Appearance

Characteristics such as size and temperament are more or less standard from one goblin to the next. When it comes to the details of their appearance, however, goblins do not have much in common. Sources even disagree about the type of animal a goblin most closely resembles. According to the present-day Spiderwick series, for example, goblins look a great deal like toads. In pictures drawn by Spiderwick artist DiTerlizzi, these goblins have large mouths, long tongues, and squat bodies. On the other hand, goblins in another fantasy series look much more like bats than like toads, and a traditional story from Japan features a goblin that is indistinguishable from a very large rat.

Tiny goblins offer up fresh-picked grapes and other luscious fruit in this illustration of "The Goblin Market," a story by nineteenth-century English poet Christina Rossetti. While goblins have no standard features, they are most often described as small in stature.

Other goblins, however, bear a much closer resemblance to people than to any other animal. Goblins in many Scandinavian folktales tend to look much like miniature people. They usually have recognizable arms and legs, and their heads are shaped more or less like those of human beings. Several role-playing games picture goblins with human-type features, but wrapped in a sort of armor that exaggerates their strength. And in the fantasy novel *Kringle* by Tony Abbott, goblins look like short, skinny men with elongated heads and unusually sharp teeth.

Even when goblins are the same basic shape, their physical characteristics can often be highly dissimilar. Features as minor as feet vary considerably from one story to another. In MacDonald's *The Princess and the Goblin*, for instance, a human character discovers that goblins have small, soft feet. The feet of the goblins in Tolkien's *The Hobbit*, on the other hand, are large and flat. A Japanese tale describes goblins "with feet like the claws of birds."[9] And Petty equips the goblins in his novel *The Hobgoblin Proxy* with hooves.

The builds and facial features of goblins are often different as well. Petty's goblins are "skinny and shriveled"—so scrawny that, as Petty puts it, they appear to "have spent a century eating nothing but mosquitoes who happened to be sucking [them] dry."[10] One of MacDonald's characters, in direct contrast, is a goblin king who is four feet high and three and a half feet wide. Goblin eyes may be red as fire or black as coal; they may be set side by side, or vertically. As for ears, the goblins in Abbott's novel *Kringle* have "long, deep ears the color of boiled cabbage,"[11] while other goblins have tiny ears, enormous ears, or no ears at all. The variations in human bodies are nothing compared to the variations among goblins.

Other physical features also can be quite different from one goblin to the next. Some goblins have one tail, others two, and still oth-

> ## Did You Know?
> According to the Spiderwick fantasy series, some goblins mark their territory like dogs, by urinating along the boundaries.

Goblins in Dungeons and Dragons

The game Dungeons and Dragons was among the first widely popular role-playing games, and it has had an enormous influence on nearly all role-playing games developed since. In the game, as in many others like it, players take on the parts of different fantastical beings, among them dragons, gnomes, and elves. Goblins are characters in the Dungeons and Dragons games as well. Like goblins of traditional folklore, these goblins are described as small and hideously ugly. The Dungeons and Dragons goblins, moreover, are rarely given much respect by other beings. They are often described as annoying in daily life and as cowardly in battle. In these respects, the goblins of Dungeons and Dragons mirror many of the characteristics traditionally attributed to goblins.

As Dungeons and Dragons has become more complex, however, new types of goblins have been introduced—goblins not found in other sources. Snow goblins, aquatic goblins, and jungle goblins, for example, are all a part of Dungeons and Dragons updates and spinoffs of the 2000s. These and other goblins live in places, such as the Arctic, where goblins traditionally do not venture. Similarly, they may fly, swim, or otherwise travel in ways that goblins of folklore and most fantasy novels do not. The goblins of Dungeons and Dragons, then, often represent something entirely new in the goblin world.

ers three. Some have horns. Others do not. Some have long fingers, some have fingers that are short and stubby, some have claws where fingers would ordinarily be. It is not clear whether the variations have to do with different species of goblins, or whether other factors are at work. What *is* clear is that identifying a goblin based on its looks alone can be very difficult.

Home Sweet Home

Just as sources disagree about the physical features of goblins, they also disagree when it comes to the places where goblins live. Many stories tell of goblins that take up residence in houses or other buildings belonging to human beings. In a story from Denmark, for instance, the goblin lives in the basement of a grocery store. A Scottish legend, known as "The Lass Who Couldn't Be Frightened," tells of a goblin that lives under a grain mill. And in the Japanese story "The Boy Who Drew Cats," the goblin makes its home in a temple. Other goblins live under floorboards or in holes in the walls of people's houses.

Though these goblins choose to live near people, a few goblins build homes of their own. Many of these homes resemble human houses, though of course they are sized for goblins rather than for people. The Italian legend "The Three Silver Balls" describes one of these houses in detail. The home's features include a first-floor hallway, a winding staircase, a kitchen, and a large cellar. To the casual observer, the size of the house is all that distinguishes it from an ordinary house occupied by human beings.

Goblins that live indoors, however, are outnumbered by those that live in the natural world. Some, like the Erlking, make their homes in the forest. These goblins spend much of their time lurking behind bushes and awaiting opportunities to make trouble. However, forest goblins do not always remain hidden. Groups of forest goblins often gather together in small open meadows between the trees. In the French legend "Papa Greatnose," a goblin gathering offers a chance for the goblins to have some fun. Given the temperament of goblins, though, gatherings like these are more frequently used to form a goblin army or to plot mischief. In

Did You Know?

While most sources agree that goblins like music and verse, a few strongly disagree. The goblins in George MacDonald's fantasy novel *The Princess and the Goblin*, for example, despise singing and poetry.

Barry Yourgrau's story "Goblins and Their Crimes," for example, goblins assemble at night in the forest to discuss how to take revenge on a writer who they believe has written nasty and untrue things about them. "Okay, everybody," says the goblin High Fellow at the end of the meeting, when those present have agreed on a plan of action, "here be-eth the slimeball's address, let-eth's go-eth get him!"[12]

Though some goblins prefer the forests, the majority of goblins live underground, deep inside mountains or far below the surface of the earth. In both fantasy fiction and traditional folktales, goblins commonly live in subterranean towns reminiscent of prairie dog villages. The goblins may make use of natural caves and tunnels, or

Unlike their counterparts in many stories, the goblins of Tony DiTerlizzi and Holly Black's Spiderwick Chronicles *bear a strong resemblance to toads. The goblins, pictured here in a scene from the 2008 movie, have large mouths, long tongues, and squat bodies.*

they may hollow out rooms and passageways with picks and shovels. Most sources agree that goblins are quite skilled at creating living space in these places.

Night and Day

Part of the reason that many goblins choose to live below the ground involves safety. Most of these goblin lairs are well away from humans and other potentially dangerous creatures, and the entrances are often difficult to find. "[Goblins] can tunnel and mine as well as any but the most skilled dwarves,"[13] Tolkien explains in *The Hobbit*. This skill gives goblins an enormous advantage over those who might try to attack them. By constructing a complex network of tunnels and underground rooms and committing the pathways to memory, goblins can defend themselves easily against enemies who manage to make their way inside their mountains.

Goblins also like the interior of mountains because they enjoy the dark. In part, this is because they are not well adapted to sunlight. Most sources agree that goblins suffer when they are outdoors during the day. One of the mountain-dwelling goblins in *The Princess and the Goblin* calls the sun "a most disagreeable contrivance . . . intended no doubt to blind us when we venture out under its baleful influence!"[14] The sun is no mere annoyance to many goblins, however. Some legends claim that goblins will be turned to stone if the sun ever shines on them. Stories like these are more often associated with trolls than with goblins in traditional folklore, but several folk stories describe how goblins are turned to stone when they forget to be careful—or are unavoidably delayed on their way back home. This theme is especially common in Dutch folklore, for example.

> ## Did You Know?
>
> Nearly all goblins in folktales, fantasy fiction, and role-playing games are male. Among the few female goblins who play an important role in goblin literature is a powerful goblin named Zitzie, who appears in the movie *Labyrinth* and its spinoffs.

Because of their difficulties with sunlight, most goblins are nocturnal: Like bats, owls, and some kinds of foxes, they sleep during the day and are most energetic at night. The goblin that lives beneath the grain mill in the Scottish tale "The Lass Who Couldn't Be Frightened" pays little attention to people when the sun is up. Though the reason is not stated directly, it is most likely because it is asleep. After sunset, though, the situation is quite different. "If anyone tries to grind any flour at night," the miller explains, "[the goblin] comes out and steals it and gives [the person] a good thrashing."[15] Not surprisingly, the people of the village avoid the mill between dusk and dawn, when the goblin is most likely to be active.

Not all goblins are afraid of sunlight, however. Nor are goblins necessarily nocturnal. Folklore and fantasy fiction are full of stories of goblins that are perfectly happy venturing out during the day and seem to suffer no particular consequences from doing so. An eastern European story called "Water Drops" takes place during the day, for example. So does Molly Bang's retelling of the East Asian folktale "The Goblins Giggle." Though night-loving goblins are much more common than goblins that move around during the day, it is not safe to assume that goblins never come out in daytime. A creature that looks something like a goblin may very well be one, even if the sun is high in the sky.

Goblins and Food

Just as sources disagree about what goblins use for shelter, sources also do not see eye to eye about goblins and their relationship to food. According to MacDonald's novel *The Princess and the Goblin*, goblins rarely eat. "*We* can go for a week at a time without food, and be all the better for it," remarks the goblin king, "but I've been told that *they* [that is, humans] eat two or three times every day!"[16] According to Tolkien, though, exactly the opposite is true. "Goblins," he wrote in 1937, "are always hungry."[17] Either MacDonald and Tolkien were describing different species of goblins, or goblins grew much more interested in food between the 1870s and the late 1930s.

Goblins of the Silver Screen

Most goblins appear in books and stories. Some, however, have been important characters in movies over the years. The 1994 animated feature *The Princess and the Goblin*, for example, is based on George MacDonald's fantasy novel of the same name. The three Lord of the Rings movies, released between 2001 and 2003 and including goblins as characters, are adaptations of J.R.R. Tolkien's novels. And the 1986 film *Labyrinth*, which features singer David Bowie as the king of the goblins, was influenced by Maurice Sendak's popular picture book *Outside over There*.

Portraying goblins in live action movies can be difficult. Designers and directors are limited to makeup and costuming that can realistically be applied to the human body. Nonetheless, the goblins that appear in these films add to our understanding of what these creatures can look like. For his role as the goblin king in *Labyrinth*, for example, Bowie appears onscreen with long blond hair, upturned eyebrows, and a scar on his left cheek. Befitting the advances in technology over the next two decades, the portrayal of the orcs, or goblins, in the Lord of the Rings movies is much more sophisticated—and less obviously human—than Bowie's goblin king. The orc Shagrat, for example, has mismatched eyes, a deeply wrinkled face, and a mouth filled with teeth more like those of an ape than of a man.

As for the question of what goblins eat, the short answer appears to be that they eat everything they can find. Some show a particular fondness for the food eaten by humans. The folktale "The Cook and the House Goblin," for example, tells of a goblin that is extremely hungry for the stew a cook is preparing. Other stories say that, among other delicacies, goblins like cream, cherries, jam, and wine. And several tales tell of goblins that show up uninvited at feasts planned and prepared by humans. Once at the feasts, the goblins swarm all over the tables, eating as much as they can hold.

But in the absence of human food, goblins are perfectly content to eat other things. Many tales claim that goblins eat large animals, such as horses. In some cases, they eat just the flesh of these creatures, but more often they gnaw away at the entire carcass, bones and all. Some goblins eat what humans would consider garbage. And most goblins are extremely fond of the taste of human beings. Indeed, the central focus of many stories about goblins is the goblins' attempt to catch and eat people.

Wealth, Weapons, and Music

According to legend, goblins spend most of their time engaged in one of two activities: Either they are planning murder and mischief or they are carrying it out. Goblins do have several other interests and skills, however. Most goblins, though not all, are very interested in money. The ruler of the goblins, reports a Dutch fairy tale, lives in an underground palace that is "made of gold and glitter[s] with gems."[18] A German folktale tells of a goblin community where the bathtubs are made of gold and the buttons on the clothes are made of pearl. Many goblins also spend time trying to increase their wealth. In several stories, the goblins' main work is tunneling through underground mines in search of precious metals.

> **Did You Know?**
>
> Goblins cannot easily be distinguished from their close cousins, the equally short brownies, pixies, and gremlins.

Goblins also frequently turn their attention to the manufacture of tools, including weapons. Among creatures of fantasy, dwarves are usually considered the most capable craftsmen, able to make extremely complicated objects out of silver, iron, and other metals. But if dwarves represent the highest level, goblins are not far behind. "They make no beautiful things, but they make many clever ones,"

writes Tolkien. "Hammers, axes, swords, daggers, pickaxes, tongs, and also instruments of torture, they make very well."[19]

According to many sources, music is another common interest among goblins. Many goblins are very fond of singing, though their voices are annoying and the words of their songs are frequently gibberish. "Skree skree skraaaagh,"[20] croak the goblins in a Japanese tale, while a human character nearby hides, hoping not to be noticed. Songs with actual lyrics tend to be nasty and cruel. "Swish, smack! Whip crack!" sing Tolkien's goblins after taking the main characters of *The Hobbit* prisoner. "Batter and beat! Yammer and bleat!"[21] The noise is horrible, the story's narrator reports, and the words are punctuated by malicious laughter and the sound of whips slapping onto the captives' backs.

Goblins and Magic

Goblins' ability to use magic is yet another area where legends and traditions differ. To some degree, of course, goblins are by their very nature magic. Along with ogres, vampires, fairies, and other legendary beings, goblins are part of the supernatural world. Still, many stories of the supernatural emphasize that goblins are not subject to the laws of physics.

One common example involves travel. According to many legends, goblins can move from one place to another in a fraction of a second, no matter the distance. A legend from India describes a human king who finds a goblin by a tree and takes it prisoner. The king begins to carry the goblin back to his palace, but the goblin has other ideas: It returns in an instant to the tree, and the king must travel back to recapture it.

Goblins are also occasionally described as shape-shifters—that is, creatures with the ability to change their form at will. According to Japanese folklore, for instance, some goblins have the shape of small spiders most of the time but can adopt human form as well. An English song dating from the early 1600s describes a goblin called Robin Goodfellow, boasting that it can appear to others in a variety of animal forms. "Sometimes I meet them like a man [that is, in human form]," Goodfellow reports, "sometimes an oxe, sometimes a hound."[22]

Legends and fantasy fiction often endow goblins with other magical powers, too. In Abbott's novel *Kringle* the goblins own a special wand, an iron staff called Ithgar. "Ithgar," writes Abbott, "held power over the wind and snow and ice. . . . Using Ithgar, the goblins had learned to conjure storms."[23] A

> ## Did You Know?
> Shiva, an important god in the Hindu tradition, is often depicted in the middle of a group of goblins that serve as assistants.

Dutch tale called "The Goblins Turned to Stone" asserts that goblins can turn themselves invisible with the help of magical red caps. And in a traditional Greek legend a goblin removes its eyes and tosses them high into the air; this allows it to see much of the world in an instant.

But not all sources agree that goblins have any particular magical abilities. Though some goblins can travel as fast as they like, many others move at roughly the same speed as humans and other nonmagical creatures. Most goblin rulers appear to lack magic wands, and relatively few goblins have the power to turn invisible. As with many other characteristics, magical powers are not shared by all goblins.

Beware of Goblins Lurking

Always hungry or almost never hungry; living under floorboards or in fancy goblin-sized homes; the possessors of one pair of eyes, two pairs of eyes, or no eyes whatsoever—the variation among goblins is as great as it is among any other creatures on Earth, and perhaps beyond. This variation can present a significant problem for those who want to learn more about goblins—as well as for those who seek only to avoid them. It may be simple to identify a vampire by sight or to compile a short but thorough guide to the habits of leprechauns. To do the same for goblins, though, requires extensive study. Still, given the murderous nature of quite a few goblins, people are well advised to take the time to do this research before venturing to a place where goblins may be lurking.

Chapter 2

Killers, Kidnappers, and Orcs: Goblins of Malice

Few goblins could be described as pleasant company. But some goblins are nastier than others. The worst of the goblins are those whose main goal in life is to harm people. These cruel and vengeful beings stage surprise raids on human houses in the darkness; they seize unwary travelers in the forests at night; they steal human babies from their cradles when no one is looking. Many are murderous creatures who seek to destroy their enemies, often in as painful a fashion as possible. These are the goblins of malice. As story after story demonstrates, it is wise to stay as far away from them as possible.

Murderous Goblins

Quite a few mythological creatures are dangerous to humans. According to legend, ogres—large hairy beings with powerful jaws and an angry disposition—frequently seek out people in order to eat them. When in their wolf form, werewolves can use their claws and sharp teeth to kill a person. Vampires suck the blood from human beings, sometimes killing their victims in the process. And a host of other legendary beings, from dragons to the Minotaur and from giants to hags, not only *can* kill people—but often do.

In some very important ways, goblins are not much like these fantastical creatures. Most notably, of course, the typical goblin is much smaller than the typical giant, werewolf, or vampire. Goblins, moreover, lack the ability to breathe fire, like dragons do, and they are much less muscular than ogres. Their smaller size and strength,

Bloodthirsty goblins known as orcs populate J.R.R. Tolkien's fantasy worlds. Orcs wage war in this scene from the 2001 movie The Lord of the Rings: The Fellowship of the Ring.

along with their inability to suck blood or breathe fire, might suggest that goblins could not possibly be as dangerous as these other beings.

To assume that, however, would be a serious and perhaps fatal mistake. Stories demonstrate time and again that goblins intent on causing havoc can be every bit as harmful as the most vicious hags or werewolves. From traditional folktales to modern fantasy fiction, those who underestimate the power and wickedness of goblins almost always regret it.

Murderous goblins appear in legends from a variety of cultures, as well as in stories spun by fantasy authors from the nineteenth century to the present. One of the most ferocious of goblins in all literature is the Erlking. The Erlking and other goblins like it lurk in the woods at night, waiting for unsuspecting travelers to pass by. When it sees a small person, such as a child, it leaps from the forest cover and attacks. Most of the time the Erlking's intent is to kill its victims.

Rarely is a reason given for the Erlking's hostility to people. It is simply an evil creature who enjoys terrifying those who pass by its home at night.

Several goblins of fantasy and myth, likewise, are noted for trying to lure people to their deaths. The folklore of Scotland, for example, includes mentions of goblins called spunkies. According to legend, spunkies spend most of their time lurking in wild places on foggy nights. They carry lanterns that cast light. When travelers come by, the spunkies hold the lights high in the air, hoping to fool the travelers into thinking that the lights represent a house, a bridge, or some other sign of civilization. Travelers who follow the source of the light come to a tragic end. The spunkies lead their victims off the path and into the wilderness—and eventually over the edge of a cliff.

> ## Did You Know?
>
> In the long, creepy 1862 poem "The Goblin Market" by English poet Christina Rosetti, goblins feed poisoned fruits to two sisters in an attempt to kidnap them.

"The Boy Who Drew Cats"

Perhaps the best known of all bloodthirsty goblins is a character in a Japanese folktale called "The Boy Who Drew Cats." The story deals with a boy who is training to be a priest. Though the boy is

The Spider Goblin

One of the sneakiest of all goblins is a figure from Japanese folklore known as a spider goblin (or sometimes a goblin spider). This creature takes the form of an ordinary spider most of the time, but can shape-shift into a human whenever it wants. In a traditional story about this creature, a samurai, or Japanese warrior, determines to rid the world of a particularly bloodthirsty goblin spider. Accordingly, he spends the night in a temple known to be one of the creature's favorite haunts.

Late in the night, a priest arrives at the temple and begins to play a song on a musical instrument. The song is so beautiful that the samurai immediately suspects that the priest is not a real man but the goblin in human form. No human, he reasons, could play that beautifully. He raises his sword to kill the priest, but the priest begins to laugh. "So you thought I was a goblin?" he chides the warrior. "Oh no! I am only a priest of this temple; but I have to play to keep [away] the goblins."

Embarrassed, the samurai starts to apologize—only to have the priest suddenly turn into a spider and encase him in an enormous web. In the end, with help from nearby villagers, the samurai is able to escape and kill the goblin. Still, the goblin's actions show the level of deviousness these creatures are capable of.

Lafcadio Hearn, *The Goblin Spider*. Tokyo: T. Hasegawa, 1926.

intelligent and obedient, he has an odd compulsion: drawing pictures of cats. "He drew them on the margins of the priest's books," reads one retelling of the story, "and on all the screens of the temple, and on the walls, and on the pillars."[24] Worse yet, he draws when he should be studying.

Tiring of this behavior, the priest who is in charge of the boy's education sends him away. Ashamed to go home, the boy travels instead to another temple in a nearby town. What the boy does not know is that a vicious goblin has taken over the temple and all attempts to reclaim it have failed. Those who tried have all been killed and eaten by the goblin.

When the boy reaches the temple, he is surprised to find it empty. He believes that the priests will come back soon, so he settles down to wait. While the boy waits, he draws a number of cats on some nearby blank screens. At last, the exhausted boy curls up inside a small cupboard and falls asleep.

In the middle of the night the boy is suddenly awakened by an awful noise—the screams and sounds of a terrible fight. The boy burrows deeper into the cabinet and only comes out when the battle is long since over and the sun has come up. Then, as American writer Lafcadio Hearn describes it in an early telling of the story, "The first thing he saw was that all the floor of the temple was covered with blood. And then he saw, lying dead in the middle of it, an enormous, monstrous rat—a goblin-rat—bigger than a cow!"[25] As he looks around the temple, the boy sees that the cats he drew the previous evening all have bright red stains around their mouths. During the night, he realizes, the cats came to life and killed the evil goblin.

> ## Did You Know?
> Some especially blood-thirsty goblins that live on old battlefields are sometimes called redcaps because they dip their hats in the blood of dead soldiers.

The Most Fearsome Enemy

As is demonstrated by the Erlking, the spunkies, and the ratlike goblin of "The Boy Who Drew Cats," individual goblins can be formidable opponents. Even so, goblins are most dangerous when they form packs. Many stories tell of whole goblin armies swarming through forests, tunnels, and buildings. Even when their opponents manage to kill five, 10, or even several dozen goblins, the advantage in numbers is almost impossible to overcome. When hundreds or thousands of goblins are in a single group, a small band of people, dwarves, or other creatures cannot fight them all off for long.

This is quite clear in the case of the goblins that inhabit Tolkien's fantasy world, Middle Earth. This world is described in Tolkien's classic novel *The Hobbit* and again in his *Lord of the Rings* trilogy. These books each feature a group of travelers, typically including dwarves, elves, the good wizard Gandalf, and the small peace-loving creatures that Tolkien called hobbits. These characters are the heroes of the works. They are on a quest, and in each book they must overcome a variety of dangerous creatures to reach their goal. Most of these creatures are unpleasant; again and again the travelers barely escape death at the hands of their enemies.

No Middle Earth enemy is more fearsome or more alarming than the goblins, known sometimes as orcs in Tolkien's works. Part of the reason is temperament. Middle Earth's goblins are bloodthirsty, ready to kill at the slightest provocation. Worse yet, Tolkien's goblins have special skills that help them greatly in finding and killing their victims. They are excellent at making weapons, and they have a powerful sense of smell that enables them to track their prey many hours or days after their victims have passed by.

Captured by Goblins

The Middle Earth goblins appear for the first time early in *The Hobbit*, when the travelers pass along the slopes of the mountains in which the goblins live. While spending the night in what they think is a cave, the characters wake up to see their ponies and equipment being carried away through a small crack in the wall of the cave. They quickly realize that the cave is not a cave at all but the opening of a tunnel dug by the goblins. But before they can react, the goblins seize them, wrap them in chains, and carry them down into the mountain.

The outlook is bleak for the travelers at this point. The Great Goblin, the head of the band, is not inclined to treat them gently.

"Slash them!" it cries. "Beat them! Bite them! Gnash them! Take them away to dark holes full of snakes, and never let them see the light again!"[26] Thanks largely to the magic of the wizard Gandalf, the travelers do manage to escape, but the goblins pursue them, as do the goblins' allies, bloodthirsty wolflike creatures known as Wargs. Though the travelers narrowly evade the Wargs by climbing trees just ahead of the animals' snapping jaws, the goblins appear shortly afterward and start setting fires at the bases of the trees.

The Belief in Changelings

The notion of a changeling springs partly from long-standing human beliefs in spirits and fantastical monsters. It has another important origin, too. That is the existence throughout history of children with birth defects and rare diseases. For purely medical reasons, these children may look extremely odd at birth; their heads may be swollen, for instance, they may be missing fingers or a leg; their skin color may be markedly lighter or darker than usual. Likewise, children may not develop normally through their early years. They may never acquire language, for example, or may have trouble learning to walk or coordinate their muscles.

Today, we recognize these problems as medical issues. Doctors know about conditions such as cystic fibrosis, autism, and spina bifida, among many others that can affect children. In earlier times, though, people had much less medical knowledge than they do today. No one knew what caused a child to be born with deformed feet or to cry constantly as an infant. The belief in changelings was one way of making sense of these children: In this view, the children were not the actual offspring of their supposed parents, but children of another type of being altogether, substituted for parents' happy, healthy children without their knowledge.

The travelers can see no possible way out. The goblins begin a dance around the fires, singing about what they plan to do when the group is forced to descend. "What shall we do with the funny little things?" they sing. "Roast 'em alive, or stew them in a pot; Fry them, boil them, and eat them hot?"[27] That the travelers will be eaten seems clear—and just as before, no escape seems possible. Luckily for the travelers, though, they are saved once again. This time an army of eagles flies by and drives the goblins away. The eagles then carry the travelers to safety.

Goblin Brides

Even when evil goblins do not try to kill their victims, they are still powerful and dangerous. According to legends widespread in Europe and elsewhere, goblins often try to kidnap people and carry them away. In one story, known in much of eastern Europe, a young woman is completing her work late one night when she is accosted by a group of goblins in a fine coach pulled by four handsome horses. The goblins are dressed in fancy, formal clothing, as if they are about to go to a wedding. As it turns out, this is exactly their intention. "Your bridegroom awaits you!" one of the goblins calls to the woman, according to one retelling of the story. "I have chosen you as wife for one of my sons."[28]

Though the woman is terrified and shocked to hear the goblins' plans, the story has a happy ending. Knowing that the goblins cannot remain above the ground past dawn, the woman explains that she will need several items of clothing in order to be a bride beautiful enough to suit her new goblin husband. Then she lists the items one by one, as slowly as possible. The goblins move extremely quickly, but time nevertheless passes as they gather the dress, shoes, and other clothes the young woman requests. In the end the woman manages to delay her departure until dawn, and the goblins vanish just as the sun comes up. Still, the cruelty of the goblins is evident in their willingness to sacrifice the woman's happiness for their own selfish goals.

Princess Irene, one of the title characters in MacDonald's fantasy *The Princess and the Goblin*, is a target of a similar attack. The princess lives in a palace located near an entire community of mountain-dwelling goblins. The goblin king wants to find a bride for his son Harelip and decides that he will kidnap Princess Irene to become Harelip's wife.

The plot to capture Irene goes quite well at first. Working in secret, the goblins tunnel all the way to the palace and break into the cellar. The cellar appears to be unguarded, and the goblins think they have carried the day. "In a moment the goblin royal family and the whole goblin people were on their way in hot haste to the [human] king's house," MacDonald writes, "each eager to have a share in the glory of carrying off that same night the Princess Irene."[29]

However, the attack is not as much of a surprise as the goblins believe. A miner named Curdie has been tracking the goblins' progress, and he and some other humans beat back the goblins when they try to climb the steps into the main part of the palace. Many goblins are killed, and the survivors run back into the mountain. Thanks to Curdie's heroism, Princess Irene escapes becoming a goblin's bride.

Children

When they are looking for a bride, goblins steal just one person. Where children are concerned, though, they may try to steal hundreds. In the novel *Kringle* by Tony Abbott, for instance, the title character enters an enormous underground cavern that he knows is inhabited by goblins. But while Kringle expects to see goblins, he does not expect to see children—and the cavern, as it turns out, is full of children, each of them kidnapped by the goblins. "All were in rags," Abbott writes, "and all [were] chained by their ankles or wrists or both. They were huddled together in fear, surrounded by a numberless army of hissing black goblins, larger red goblins, and the usual green ones."[30] In all, Kringle learns, at least 500 children are in the cavern, and more are being captured every day.

The purpose of stealing children varies from one story to the next. Some goblins take children who have been disobedient. One especially lethal example is a goblin known as Bloody Bones. One modern author describes Bloody Bones as "a hideous crouching figure with blood running down his face, his hair matted with filth and blood, sitting on a pile of bones." Not surprisingly, given a description like that, Bloody Bones eats children—but not just any children. He lurks below staircases and inside cupboards, waiting for "naughty children who tell lies and say bad words."[31] These children do not live to tell about their experiences. Instead, they quickly become Bloody Bones's lunch.

The story of Bloody Bones can be used as a cautionary tale for children who misbehave. It can also be told as a ghost tale, designed to give listeners, especially children, a delicious shiver of fear. In either case, Bloody Bones is one of several goblins who spirit children away because of something the child did.

More often, however, goblins steal children for reasons of their own. Sometimes the goblins are in search of servants or slaves. Alternatively they hold the prisoners for ransom, or keep them as hostages. The goblin king in *The Princess and the Goblin* is not just interested in providing his son with a bride; he is eager to capture Princess Irene as a sort of insurance policy. He plans to make demands on the humans once he has Irene under his control. If the humans do not agree to give the goblin what he wants, he will threaten to hurt or even kill the princess.

Changelings

While goblins are happy to capture children of any age, they take particular pleasure in spiriting away babies. They are especially fond of leaving a living creature in its place. Usually these creatures are the actual offspring of the goblins that are making the change, but sometimes they are other beings altogether. These substitute babies are known as changelings. Stories about changelings are widespread in the folklore of northern Europe, especially in parts of the British Isles. Goblins are not the only mythological creature to substitute changelings for babies—trolls and several other small supernatural monsters do so as well—but goblins are heavily involved in the changeling business.

It might seem that parents would notice right away once a substitution has been made. But in fact that is not always true. During the first few days after a substitution, parents often have no idea

> ## Did You Know?
>
> A weird sea creature found off the coast of Japan is called the goblin shark because of its frightening, goblinlike facial features, including a pointed snout, long and powerful jaws, and sharp teeth.

that anything unusual has happened. Evidently the resemblance between baby goblins and baby humans is considerably closer than the resemblance between adult goblins and humans. Some stories also refer to magic spells that make the changelings appear more like people.

But as the changelings grow, it becomes increasingly impossible to deny that something is wrong. The babies may start to develop large goblinlike heads, and their faces often become ugly and grotesque. Some changelings have unusually pale skin, while the skin of others begins to appear greenish. Changelings may talk extremely early, or extremely late, or not at all. As one character reports in Petty's fantasy novel *The Hobgoblin Proxy*, goblins replace human babies "with clay changelings that fool the mother until they wash away with the bathwater."[32] When this happens, of course, no one can any longer deny that a changeling has been substituted for the real baby. The evidence of a dissolved child is indisputable.

Revenge, Malice, and More

A goblin, troll, or other fantastical being might substitute a changeling for a human baby for a number of reasons. One is revenge: Goblins often substitute changelings for the children of people who have wronged them in the past. Another is to provide a steady supply of servants or slaves for goblin families. A third, however, is simple malice. Even if goblins that substitute changelings for human babies have no particular desire to kill people, they nevertheless do not want humans to be happy. By replacing a beloved child with a baby goblin or a magical lump of clay, they cause extreme pain at little cost or danger to themselves. Given the basic temperament of goblins, especially goblins of evil, this motive is perhaps the most compelling of all.

According to both folklore and fantasy fiction, parents can do little to avoid the substitution of a changeling for a baby. A few legends claim that goblins are afraid of iron, so placing iron near a child's cradle will help keep the baby safe. Other sources, however, dismiss this notion as false. Similarly, stories sometimes assert that by staying beside the baby at all times, a parent can protect it from being kidnapped. Once again, though, other tales insist that the substitution of a changeling for a baby happens so quickly that a human being is unlikely to notice. Even if a parent could stay awake for months, never leaving the child's side, these stories claim, a goblin would have no trouble making the substitution.

Nor can a parent do much once the substitution has taken place. Generally speaking, once the baby has disappeared, it will never be seen again. That being said, a few stories do describe how families get their children back. In one traditional German story, a mother is advised to boil water in eggshells while the changeling watches. The ridiculousness of the sight will make the changeling laugh, the mother is told, and the laughter will force the goblins to return to her house and exchange the babies again. That is exactly what happens, and the mother is able to reclaim her own child.

A more recent example is Maurice Sendak's picture book *Outside over There*, published in 1981. In this story, written in the style of a folktale, goblins have stolen the baby sister of a girl named Ida. "They pushed their way in and pulled [the] baby out," Sendak explains, "leaving another all made of ice."[33] Ida recognizes the substitution when the baby made of ice begins to melt. She goes off on a journey to locate her little sister and comes to the place where the goblins are keeping the baby. By playing music on her horn for the goblins, she gets them to dance. They dance hard enough that they eventually turn to water, like the changeling, and Ida is able to reclaim her baby sister.

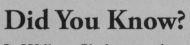

Did You Know?

In William Shakespeare's play *Hamlet*, a ghost appears to the title character. Hamlet wonders aloud whether the ghost is a kindly spirit or an evil goblin from the depths of hell.

But although taking back a child that has been kidnapped by goblins is possible, no one can guarantee that a parent—or a big sister—will actually be able to do so. Nor can anyone guarantee that a hobbit caught by malevolent goblins will be saved at the last moment by the intervention of a wizard, or be certain that cats sketched on a screen, no matter how elaborately drawn, will protect a boy from a goblin in the shape of a rat. The goblins of malice in this world, and in other worlds as well, are best left alone. While these goblins can be defeated, the risks are enormous—and the cost of failure may be fatal.

Chapter 3

Pranksters, Thieves, and Pinchers: Goblins of Mischief

The most famous goblins are the murderous kind. Goblins such as Bloody Bones, the Erlking, and the goblins of Tolkien's Middle Earth get most of the attention from fantasy fans and folklorists, and rightly so. These goblins, after all, are the heavy hitters of goblindom. They are the ones that people must avoid when traveling through foggy forests, spending the night in deserted temples, or seeking shelter on mountain slopes. Just as murder is a bigger story on the nightly news than burglary or making illegal right turns, so too are the best-known goblins the ones who are the most dangerous.

But homicidal goblins are less common than the attention given to them might indicate. Despite the very real danger of being killed or kidnapped by a goblin bent on causing humans as much pain as possible, these goblins are actually fairly rare. Most goblins, in fact, do not seem terribly interested in killing anyone. Their main goal in life, instead, is to be annoying—to break things, to create messes, and to disturb the peace and quiet of people who live near them. These are the goblins of mischief, and they appear regularly in stories of the imaginary world.

Practical Jokers

At heart, mischievous goblins are practical jokers. Their goal is to embarrass others and to have a laugh at someone else's expense. Their sense of humor is broad and usually very visual. They especially enjoy playing tricks in which people end up sprawled on the floor or in which a person's prized possession is broken. Upon playing a successful prank, their typical reaction is unrestrained laughter. The movies made by slapstick comedians such as the Three Stooges and Adam Sandler often include the sort of humor favored by goblins of mischief.

Mistaken identities play an important role in goblins' practical jokes. Indeed, goblins delight in pretending to be something they are not. Several legends about English goblin Robin Goodfellow, for example, mention that farmers set traps for wild animals that prey on their sheep and cows. According to these stories, Goodfellow loves to climb inside these traps and pretend to be a captured animal. The farmer is invariably delighted to see a possible predator thrashing around inside the snare. He is less happy when Goodfellow jumps out, laughs hysterically, and dashes away.

Few of the practical jokes played by goblins involve much thought. In a modern fantasy book, *The Goblin Companion*, Brian Froud and Terry Jones describe a little-known goblin named Gröeg. This goblin, according to Froud and Jones, is believed to

> ### Did You Know?
> According to some folk traditions, echoes are the work of goblins mocking people by repeating the last word of their sentences again and again.

play jokes such as "substitut[ing] margarine for the butter in the dish, or mak[ing] you think you're about to drink a cup of tea when it's really coffee."[34] Some practical jokes played by goblins seem even more juvenile. The Spiderwick series, for example, introduces readers to an adult goblin named Piddledrip. According to one passage, Piddledrip "like[s] to steal crayons and scribble all over the walls at night."[35]

As juvenile as the pranks may be, however, the goblins no doubt thoroughly enjoy their jokes. In a song dating from the early 1600s, goblin Robin Goodfellow sings about some of his favorite pranks, such as unexpectedly blowing out the candles at parties and pushing people out of bed as they sleep. Though Goodfellow's victims do not much enjoy such jokes, the little goblin himself thinks they are utterly hilarious. Each stanza of the song closes with the goblin snickering over the prank he has just pulled on some unsuspecting person. As he sings at the end of one verse, "And loudly laugh I, ho ho ho!"[36]

The characters of Piddledrip, Gröeg, and Goodfellow are by no means evil. They do not begin to approach the level of nastiness shown by Tolkien's orcs, the Erlking, or the ratlike goblin killed by the cats in the Japanese temple. On the other hand, it would be incorrect to argue that figures like Gröeg and Piddledrip wish humans well. Their sole interest lies in having fun at someone else's expense, and they see nothing wrong with causing people all sorts of difficulties in the process. This behavior is of course not particularly nice; still, any human would surely prefer a month of Robin Goodfellow's antics and washing Piddledrip's graffiti from the walls to one evening spent with the vicious and cruel goblins of Tony Abbott's *Kringle*.

Theft

Goblins of mischief are not only practical jokers; they are also highly skilled thieves. The small size of most goblins, together with their ability to move quickly but noiselessly, allows them to slip away with objects they like without being noticed. At times goblins steal because they want a specific object that is in someone else's possession. Weapons, such as knives and swords, are often included in this category. So is treasure of all kinds. No piece of gold or precious gem is ever completely safe with goblins in the neighborhood.

In the imaginary realms of literature and lore, mischievous goblins often cross over into the human world where they play practical jokes on unsuspecting people. Goblins set to work as a young woman sleeps in this nineteenth-century painting.

Goblins steal more than treasure, though. Among the more peculiar items they take are teeth. According to the Spiderwick series, goblins have no teeth of their own and must make teeth themselves or gather them from other sources. Sometimes they make do with small pieces of rock or glass. The teeth that work best, however, are actual teeth that used to be in some other creature's mouth. Since these are goblins of mischief, not goblins of evil, they do not accost people on the street or in the forest and forcibly pry the teeth from their victims' mouths. But they do often make away with the teeth that children leave under their pillows at night for the tooth fairy. This is of course frustrating for the tooth fairy but perhaps especially frustrating for the children, who are disappointed to discover that their teeth are gone—and no money has been left in exchange. Their disappointment, of course, bothers the goblins not at all.

Sometimes goblins steal objects that they can hold for ransom. One classic goblin tale from Japan deals with an object that is used as a hostage of sorts. In the story, a man stumbles upon a large group of goblins in the forest late at night. The goblins are busy performing a grotesque song and dance. Trapped and terrified, the man tries hard to stay out of sight, but the goblin king sees him and forces him to join their merrymaking. When the dance is over, the goblins urge the man to come back another time. To make sure he will obey, they decide to steal the man's favorite possession. "We'll take it and keep it until he comes back!"[37] one of the goblins cries out.

The plan is reasonable, but the goblins make a serious mistake. They notice that the man has a large, unsightly cyst growing on one cheek. The cyst is both ugly and prominent; indeed, it reminds the goblins of their own hideous faces. The goblins consequently assume that the man must be very proud of the cyst, and so they tell the man

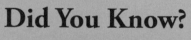

Did You Know?

In Greek folklore goblins collectively known as the *kallikantzaroi* spend most of the year underground but emerge for the Christmas season each year in order to play tricks on unsuspecting people.

World of Warcraft

The role-playing game World of Warcraft includes many fantastical characters, and goblins are among them. In the world of the game, goblins are hardy little fighters who rarely surrender and can prove extremely difficult to dislodge from a fortification. Goblins also play a role off the battlefields. Because of their technical skills and interest in money, they serve as builders and merchants who supply other characters with weapons, technology, and other items.

Like many other goblins of literature, both past and present, the goblins of World of Warcraft are also tricksters. These goblins do not trip people or play practical jokes, but their trickery comes out in other ways. Mainly they are known for cheating their customers in business deals. Trusting a World of Warcraft goblin is never a good idea when buying goods. They are noted for selling items for much more than they are worth and for passing off poorly engineered weapons and other supplies as being of high quality. Indeed, within the World of Warcraft game the expression "to cheat a goblin" has come to mean "to do the impossible."

that they will steal his cyst. Thinking quickly, the man realizes that he does not want to make them think otherwise. "This is my only treasure!" he yells, feigning panic. "Don't take it away!"[38]

The goblins pay no attention. Surrounding the defenseless man, they pull the cyst completely off his cheek. Laughing hysterically, the goblins then vanish as the terrified man falls asleep under a tree. Upon waking, the man immediately feels his face. Both cheeks feel exactly alike, just as they did before the cyst appeared. As the goblins promised, the unattractive cyst is gone. The man laughs joyfully and makes his way out of the forest and home to his family, never to return to the goblins' dances again.

Stealing Food

Along with treasure, food is certainly at the top of goblins' must-steal lists. Mischievous goblins like nothing better than taking food that belongs to someone else. Stealing food, after all, saves goblins the trouble of growing it or cooking it themselves. A poem by children's author Kate Greenaway, for instance, begins as follows:

> This fat little goblin,
> A notable sinner,
> Stole cabbages daily
> For breakfast and dinner.[39]

Greenaway's goblin knows perfectly well that its thievery angers and frustrates the farmer who planted the cabbages. But the farmer's response is of no concern to the goblin. It simply laughs and continues to take whatever it wants.

A folktale from Estonia, "Water Drops," also describes the annoying behavior of mischievous goblins who take other people's food. This story deals with a group of goblins who show up uninvited at a wedding feast. The goblins quickly take over, climbing up the pillars of the hall, sitting on the tables, and most of all eating as much as they can hold. Despite the goblins' small size, this turns out to be quite a bit. As one version of the story puts it, the goblins were "putting away more food, and that in a twinkling, than all the guests gathered in the hall could have eaten in a fortnight [two weeks]."[40]

Another European folktale, "The Cook and the House Goblin," also tells of a goblin who takes food that does not belong to it. The goblin featured in this tale lives in the kitchen of a fine house. While the cook is preparing a batch of stew one evening, the goblin creeps out from under the stove and begs for a taste. "I'm so hungry, so hungry!" the goblin tells the cook. "Just a little drop, a little drop of the gravy!"[41] The cook's first impulse is to refuse. The goblin, after all, is neither a member of the household nor an invited guest. Rather, this little goblin is much more like a mouse or an ant that lives in the home but is never welcome. In short, it is a pest.

But the cook is kindhearted and convinces himself that the goblin seems to be in great need. He offers the goblin a whole spoonful of stew. To his surprise, the goblin magically eats the entire contents of the pot in just a few seconds. Before the cook can react, the goblin has scurried away beneath the oven, where of course the cook cannot follow. As is so often true in stories about mischievous goblins, the goblin in this tale eats its fill—on food prepared by somebody else.

The Hinky Pink

A few mischievous goblins are neither thieves nor practical jokers. Instead, they create havoc to get what they want. A classic example of this type of goblin stars in an old Italian folktale sometimes called "The Hinky Pink." In this story, a girl—known as Anabel in one recent retelling—is assigned the task of making a dress for a princess. The princess plans to wear the dress to an upcoming fancy ball. Anabel is excited by the opportunity to create a beautiful gown. She imagines the pride she will feel when the princess walks into the ballroom wearing the dress she made.

But the job is much more difficult than Anabel anticipates. The problem is not the dress itself, but what happens when she is ready to get some sleep. The first night something too small to be seen pinches her again and again while she lies in bed. Whatever is doing the pinching also pulls the bedcovers off Anabel. Each time she retrieves the covers and remakes the bed, it happens again. Naturally enough, Anabel gets very little sleep that night, and what sleep she gets is not very refreshing. The same thing happens on the following nights as well. Weary from lack of rest and aching from the constant

> # Did You Know?
>
> The sudden disappearance of cats and dogs from an area is often taken as an indication that goblins have moved in. Whether this is because the goblins have eaten the pets or because the pets have run to safety is not always clear.

This little fat Goblin,
  A notable sinner,
Stole cabbages daily,
  For breakfast and dinner.

The Farmer looked sorry;
  He cried, and with pain,
"That rogue has been here
  For his cabbage again!"

That little plump Goblin,
  He laughed, "Ho! ho! ha!
Before me he catches,
  He'll have to run far."

That little fat Goblin,
  He never need sorrow;
He stole three to-day,
  And he'll steal more to-morrow.

Under the Window, *Kate Greenaway's 1879 collection of pictures and rhymes for children, includes a poem about an annoying little goblin who steals cabbages from a farmer's field. The thief shows little remorse for his actions in this illustration from the book.*

pinching, Anabel has difficulty concentrating on her work. She worries that she will never be able to finish the dress.

At this point a servant diagnoses the problem. Anabel, she says, is being disturbed by a tiny species of goblin called a Hinky Pink. This type of goblin is so small it is almost impossible to see—though as Anabel has discovered, the small size of the goblin does not prevent it from inflicting great pain. The servant explains that the goblin is jealous of Anabel's big, soft bed and wants a bed of its own. Until Anabel finds the goblin an appropriate bed, the servant continues, the creature will never leave her alone.

With the deadline for the dress approaching, Anabel hurriedly sets out to accommodate the goblin. She improvises various types of beds, hoping that each attempt will meet with the goblin's approval. But each time she fails. The Hinky Pink rejects a table covered with velvet curtains (too hard), refuses to sleep on a pile of quilts that Anabel sets up in the corner (too soft), and dismisses several other makeshift beds Anabel creates.

> ## Did You Know?
>
> In Dutch folklore, goblins were often thought to cause nightmares.

Each night, once again, the goblin returns to its pinching, cover-stealing ways.

Anabel is at her wits' end when suddenly she gets an idea. Picking up a thimble from her worktable, she deftly transforms it into a tiny bed suitable for a very tiny goblin. "She lined the thimble with her silkiest satin," reads author Megan McDonald's version of the tale. "She added peach down for a pillow and a rose petal for a blanket."[42] Then Anabel places the thimble in the window and waits. Sure enough, the goblin climbs inside and finds that the bed is exactly what it wants. Anabel suffers no more pinches and no more tangled blankets. She gets a solid night's sleep, completes the dress in the morning, and presents it to the princess just in time for the ball.

Consequences

Mischievous goblins typically suffer few consequences, if any, for their thieving ways and their practical jokes. The anger felt by their victims usually subsides relatively quickly. Losing an occasional cabbage to nearby goblins, after all, is more an annoyance than a tragedy; the same is true of being fooled into eating margarine instead of butter, or of the sudden appearance of crayoned scribbles on the walls. Moreover, goblins are difficult to catch. Not only are they small, but they move quickly, and some can change their shape at will. As Greenaway's cabbage-stealing goblin notes, the farmer has only a small chance of stopping the thefts. "Before me he catches," the goblin boasts, "he'll have to run far."[43]

Some goblins, however, do get caught. Occasionally they are careless and forget to stay far enough away from humans. Sometimes they are captured by a particularly dedicated human who has devoted days or even weeks to catching the goblin. When goblins of mischief are caught, they typically receive a rather light punishment that suits the minor nature of their crimes. In "The Cook and the House Goblin," for instance, the cook eventually wearies of the goblin's repeated requests for more food—and smacks the goblin over the head with a ladle. In other tales, the mischievous goblins are evicted from the human homes where they live, but they are allowed to continue their lives elsewhere.

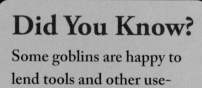

Did You Know?

Some goblins are happy to lend tools and other useful items to their human neighbors. If the tools are not returned, however, the goblins take revenge by pinching the humans.

This rule has a few exceptions. One of the most notable is the eastern European folktale "Water Drops," in which a horde of uninvited goblins shows up at a wedding feast. The goblins quickly start to eat their way through the food; it seems certain that all the food will

Goblin-Be-Gone

A magic spray or cleaning powder that can get rid of goblins easily, reliably, and cheaply does not exist. In the absence of a working Goblin-Be-Gone product, humans have needed to improvise protections and cures of their own. Some, like scaring a goblin away, work only with certain kinds of goblins, in this case ones that are already timid and unusually small. Others, like attempting to shoot a goblin or crush it in the whirling blades of a grain mill, are too heavy-handed for all but the most dangerous goblins.

One common recipe for driving mischievous goblins away from a house—a recipe used successfully in several stories about goblins—is to scatter flax seeds all over the floor. According to some authorities, goblins are superstitious and think it is bad luck not to pick up small objects like seeds where they have fallen. Before doing their mischief, then, goblins like to pick up all the seeds.

Flax seeds are very small, though, and rather slippery. That makes them difficult for goblins to locate and to corral. Under ideal circumstances, two or even three days may be needed for a goblin to pick up all the seeds. Within that time, or so the thinking goes, the goblin is apt to lose interest and move on to some other place more suitable for mischief.

be gone within a minute or two. The day is saved, though, because one of the people at the wedding has brought along a magic stick which can make things dissolve. Waving his stick at the feasting goblins, he turns them into drops of water. A few minutes later the drops are mopped up by the servants, eliminating the goblins for good.

An Ongoing Burden

Still, even the threat of being severely punished does not deter mischievous goblins from doing as they please. The goblins of fantasy fiction and folklore continue to carry out practical jokes and continue to steal what they like, regardless of the fate of the goblins in "Water Drops." Part of the reason is that goblins of mischief live very much in the moment. When these goblins have an opportunity to play a prank on someone, they take it; when they see something interesting in a forest or in a person's house, they pick it up and bring it home with them. Seldom, if ever, do they think about the consequences.

The result is predictable. From Robin Goodfellow's habit of pushing people out of bed to the Hinky Pink's enthusiastic pinches, from the goblins that steal food to the goblins that seize the teeth from below children's pillows, goblins of mischief will always be a burden for humankind. No one who lives near a goblin should expect that the mischievous activities of their neighbors will ever stop. As long as goblins live among humans, so will goblins of mischief. The best that people can do is to accept the reality of this situation— and to try to laugh along with the goblins, if at all possible.

Chapter 4

Fools, Victims, and Helpers: Good Neighbor Goblins

The majority of goblins fit neatly into one of two categories. Many are like the Erlking and the goblins that snatch babies from their cradles. These are the evil goblins, the goblins of malice, whose aim is to injure and kill other creatures. Most of the rest are like Robin Goodfellow and the goblins that eat all the food at wedding feasts. These are the goblins of mischief, the practical jokers and the petty thieves, whose purpose is to be annoying. Together, these two goblin groups include the great bulk of all goblins.

Despite these numbers, not all goblins are obnoxious or cruel. Some goblins, in fact, are essentially harmless: Though they may try to be mischievous or even evil, their attempts fall flat, putting no one in danger and causing no trouble to anyone but themselves. Many of these goblins are described as fools; even when they are carrying out practical jokes or attempting to threaten people or other creatures, their antics are silly or misguided. Readers and listeners of stories about these goblins are likely to laugh at the goblins and their lack of common sense. A few of these goblins do not lash out at anyone, except in self-defense. Instead of victimizing others with their mischief or malice, they are the innocent victims of someone else's greed, anger, or practical jokes.

Finally, some goblins are friendly, helpful, and even compassionate. While it may be difficult to believe that these goblins belong to the same species as the child-stealing goblins of Tony Abbott's *Kringle* or the murderous spunkies of Scotland, kindly goblins do indeed exist. Some of these goblins have mischievous streaks, and few are completely trustworthy. Nevertheless, together with harmless goblins, silly goblins, and a few others, these goblins form an important category: the goblins that would make reasonable next-door neighbors. Though these goblins are significantly outnumbered by the goblins of mischief and malice, they are even so a vital part of the goblin world.

> ## Did You Know?
> According to Dutch legend, goblins built the original carillon—a set of bells often found in churches and used to play music—in order to assist a local bishop who wanted more music in his cathedral.

Harmless Goblins

One important subspecies of goblins includes what might be thought of as Erlking wannabees. These are goblins that long to be as rough, tough, and mean as Bloody Bones or the goblins of Tolkien's Middle Earth. Much to their chagrin, however, these goblins are too small, too weak, or too shy to carry out any real mischief. Usually these goblins give up trying to be mischief makers by the end of the story, deciding that to be kind and gentle instead makes more sense. These goblins most often appear in stories meant for young children.

The story "The Goblins and the Fireworks" by British author Enid Blyton is one case in point. The goblins in this story decide to steal some fireworks belonging to three boys. Reluctant to treat the theft as a joke, though, the boys chase the goblins and try to reclaim their property. In this story, unlike many others, the boys have no fear of the goblins. Rather, the goblins "looked round in alarm," Blyton writes. "The boys seemed very big indeed to the tiny creatures, and the goblins were frightened."[44] The traditional roles are reversed: The goblins are scared, not the humans.

Annoying, Friendly—or Both?

Distinguishing mischievous goblins from friendly ones is usually easy. Many goblins of mischief, such as the Hinky Pink that torments Anabel the dressmaker, are clearly troublemakers: They show no sign of being helpful, friendly, or grateful. Others, such as the two goblins that assist the shoemaker in the Grimm brothers' folktale, are just as obviously friendly and helpful. For the most part, the dividing line between these two goblin types is quite apparent.

In some cases, though, the line is blurry. That is especially true with a character such as Robin Goodfellow. This goblin is primarily a trickster. Indeed, with its belly laugh and delight in embarrassing others, Goodfellow is in some ways the definition of a mischievous goblin. At the same time, Goodfellow is noted for occasionally helping people in need. "Yet now and then, the maids to please," Goodfellow announces in a song,

> I card at midnight up their wooll
>
> And while they sleep . . . with wheel to thre[a]ds their
>   flax I pull.

Goodfellow is quick to point out that this is not a common occurrence, but the fact that it happens at all is an indication that goblins are sometimes more complex creatures than they may appear at first glance.

Ballads of Robin Goodfellow, "The Mad Merry Pranks of Robin Goodfellow," Robin Hood—Bold Outlaw of Barnsdale and Sherwood. www.boldoutlaw.com.

Afraid that the boys will hurt them, but unwilling to give the fireworks back, the goblins quickly toss the firecrackers into a nearby bonfire. Of course, the fireworks go off with all manner of loud noises and sparks, which thoroughly terrifies the goblins. The boys scold the goblins for their lack of concern for other people's property and demand that the goblins repay them for the used-up fireworks. Thoroughly intimidated, the goblins are only too happy to oblige. "My goodness me," writes Blyton, "how hard those goblins worked all through that night and the next day! They ran errands for witches, they minded baby fairies for the elves. . . . And for all their hard work they were paid four pieces of silver." The goblins give the money to

Helpful goblins, less numerous in folklore and fantasy than their mean or mischievous brethren, are easily confused with other small creatures such as brownies, pixies, and fairies. Brownies celebrate in this 1880 engraving.

the boys and resolve that they will never steal anything again. "We've learnt our lesson!" says one of the goblins. "We really, really have!"[45]

Goblins of this sort are often hard to distinguish from other small creatures of legend and myth. Without a bent toward the mischievous, goblins become much like brownies, pixies, or fairies—gentler beings that also inhabit traditional folklore and fantasy worlds. Some goblins in children's poetry and fiction, in particular, behave like these other creatures. They are described more often as cute rather than mischievous, and their adventures are on the tame side. In one poem, for example, a goblin is disappointed because it is not tall enough to reach to the top of a flower—something that would not worry any self-respecting shape-shifting goblin or orc.

Goblins as Fools

Hans Christian Andersen's story "The Goblin and the Woman" features another type of goblin: one who is a figure of fun. Though Andersen's goblin is indeed mischievous, its main role in the story is to be mocked for being silly. This goblin lives in a house belonging to a woman who is a writer. Upon learning that the woman does not believe in goblins, the goblin is deeply offended. Accordingly, it sets out to convince her that she is mistaken. Rather than show itself to her, though, the goblin spends the rest of the day making mild mischief: tearing holes in her socks, making her cooking pots bubble over, and spilling cream all over the pantry floor, which it invites the woman's cat to help lick up.

The goblin changes his perception of the woman, though, when he overhears her reading a copy of her latest poem to a friend. The poem, it turns out, is called "The Little Goblin." As the goblin listens to the poem, it swells with pride: The verses describe how wonderful and powerful the goblin is, and how much the woman appreciates the role the goblin plays in her life. "I've done her wrong," thinks the goblin. "The Woman has soul and fine breeding! How I have done her wrong!"[46] It resolves to treat her kindly in the future.

What the goblin does not know, however, is that the woman's poem is not about literal goblins. Rather, it uses goblins as a metaphor for poetry. By writing about the glory of goblins, she is actually writing about the glory of poetry; when she refers to the way the goblin governs her life, she is simply stating that poetry is very important to her. The woman's cat understands this, and the reader understands it as well. The goblin, though, has no idea of the truth. The effect of the story is to make even this mischief-making goblin appear less as a prankster and more as a buffoon.

Little Jip

Occasionally tales tell of a third kind of a goblin: goblins that are innocent victims. These goblins are attacked or bothered by witches, giants, and other more powerful monsters. Usually the harassment occurs for no particular reason other than the desire of the stronger or more magical creature to push someone around. Though goblins are rarely heroes in stories, it is difficult to avoid sympathizing with the put-upon goblins featured in these tales.

One well-known example of this type of goblin is Little Jip, a character from English folklore that is very nearly eaten by a nasty witch known as One Eye. One Eye captures Little Jip twice, intending to cook the goblin, only to have it escape her clutches each time before she manages to get it home. The third time One Eye seizes Little Jip, however, the witch is more careful. One Eye brings the little goblin back to her home and goes outside to collect some firewood so she can roast it. Having seen Little Jip's ability to escape firsthand, though—and not just once, but twice—she carefully closes and locks the doors behind her.

Locking the doors is not enough, as it turns out. When One Eye comes back, Little Jip is nowhere to be seen. The goblin calls to her from the roof, explaining that it has escaped up the chimney and is

> ## Did You Know?
> Some folklorists believe that the modern-day notion of Santa Claus comes in part from the image of hobgoblins like Robin Goodfellow, a creature of boundless energy and fun who delights in laughing "ho-ho-ho."

Taking Offense

Though most goblins are happy to take rewards such as clothes and food for a job well done, they are easily offended if they are offered what they perceive to be the wrong reward for their hard work. One goblin that is especially quick to take offense in this way is a being called Kaboutermannekin, who appears in Dutch folklore. Kaboutermannekin is usually eager to help people in much the same way as the goblins helped the shoemaker: by taking on important projects such as mending fences or grinding corn in the mills at night.

This work, naturally enough, endears this little goblin to local villagers, and they are happy to reward it for its efforts. Kaboutermannekin, however, is extremely choosy about the type of rewards it will accept. It is happy to take bread, cakes, or butter, for instance, and beer is among its favorite presents. But although it is as ragged a goblin as the two that helped the shoemaker in the Grimm fairy tale, Kaboutermannekin has no interest in upgrading its wardrobe. On the contrary, if anyone attempts to give it a new suit of clothes, it takes offense and storms away, leaving the job undone. As it turns out, even the most helpful goblins are extremely touchy.

now on top of the house. "Look up the chimney and you'll see me," it assures her. One Eye stands at the bottom of the chimney, looks upward—and is struck in the head by a heavy stone that Little Jip has just dropped down the shaft. "Over she rolled, dead as a door post,"[47] reads one version of the story.

The outcome of the story makes Little Jip seem like a murderous goblin, in a category with Tolkien's orcs and other fearsome beasts. The ability of Little Jip to escape, similarly, makes it appear to be a goblin of mischief, like Robin Goodfellow or some of the goblins featured in the Spiderwick series. These analogies are not quite accurate, though. Unlike these goblins, Little Jip is defending itself against a more dangerous enemy. Its status as the underdog in the fight against the witch makes this goblin an appealing figure—and a sympathetic character in a way that is never true of, say, Tolkien's goblins. Readers of the Little Jip story usually find themselves cheering for the little goblin to defeat its enemy.

Hobgoblins

Rare are the goblins that are truly sympathetic figures, and Little Jip is one of the few. Most of the other sympathetic characters in goblin lore are helpful goblins. Often these goblins are called hobgoblins. As with many other aspects of the goblin kingdom, however, no single agreed-on definition of the term *hobgoblin* exists. In some goblin tales hobgoblins are essentially the equivalent of ordinary goblins: They share the same basic shape and temperament, but may be a few inches taller or have a better chance of becoming a leader. In some role-playing games, hobgoblins are a bit more dangerous than regular goblins, and in a few tales hobgoblins are among the nastiest goblins of them all. For example, Bloody Bones, who seizes and eats misbehaving children, is sometimes considered a hobgoblin.

Most writers, though, reserve the term *hobgoblin* to refer to a goblin that is friendlier and less dangerous than most. This usage is especially common in traditional folklore, but it is valid for many current fantasy writers as well. "I am a *hob*goblin, not a goblin," a character announces proudly in J.T. Petty's *The Hobgoblin*

Proxy. "Hobgoblins maintain order."[48] Later in the book, another character explains that hobgoblins and goblins are indistinguishable when they are born. The ones who are bad, he adds, go on to become goblins, while the ones whose behavior is exemplary grow into hobgoblins.

Whether they are called hobgoblins or not, helpful goblins certainly do exist. Unfortunately, most sources agree that it is difficult if not impossible to tell whether a goblin is a good goblin simply by its looks. The Spiderwick series, which describes mythological characters in great detail, concedes that hobgoblins are "similar to [other] goblins in appearance."[49] As a result, hobgoblins can be distinguished from their less friendly cousins only by careful observation of their activities. Luckily for the peace of mind of people who encounter goblins on a regular basis, these goblins do behave differently from the other types of goblins.

Helpful Goblins

The best-known example of hobgoblins today comes from a folktale that is not usually thought to be about hobgoblins—or, for that matter, about any sort of goblin at all. The story was collected by German brothers Jakob and Wilhelm Grimm, known today as the Brothers Grimm, who were among the first collectors of folktales. Early in the 1800s the brothers put together a fine anthology of folk and fairy tales told in and around Germany. The completed book included classics such as "Cinderella," "Snow White," and many others. It also included a story known today in English by the title "The Elves and the Shoemaker." In the Grimms' original edition, however, the story is one of three tales grouped together under the collective title "Die Wichtelmänner," or directly translated, "The Goblins."

The outline of the story is well known. The tale tells of a poor shoemaker who is on the verge of starvation. He has no money and just enough leather to make one pair of shoes. After cutting the leather into pieces of the correct shape one evening, he goes to bed. His plan is to sew the shoes together in the morning. But when he wakes up, he is astonished to see that the work has been done—and extremely well at that. He sells the resulting shoes, buys new leather, cuts out the leather for two pairs of shoes, and the process begins all over again.

Before long the shoemaker is no longer poor, and he and his wife are deeply curious about who is finishing the shoes. One evening, instead of going to bed, they conceal themselves and keep watch. Their curiosity is soon satisfied as two little goblins, dressed only in rags, enter the workshop, sew the leather into shoes, and then run off. Eager to reward the goblins but unwilling to approach them directly, the shoemaker's wife makes a tiny suit of clothing for them, and the shoemaker contributes a miniature pair of shoes for each one. When the two little goblins arrive the next evening, they are delighted to find the clothes. They dress quickly and dance out the door, never to be seen again. As for the shoemaker and his wife, in true fairy tale fashion, they live happily ever after.

> ## Did You Know?
>
> J.R.R. Tolkien used the word *hobgoblin* to apply to the largest and fiercest goblins, but later he admitted that this was a mistake caused by a misreading of English folklore. In his opinion, the term should have been applied only to generally harmless goblins.

Though this tale is the most famous story that tells of helpful goblins, other stories about goblins include similar themes. In the folktale "The Cook and the House Goblin," for instance, the goblin continually tricks the cook into giving it food. Angry that the goblin is eating so much of his dinner, the owner of the house instructs the cook to kill the goblin. But the cook is too kindhearted and cannot bring himself to do so. As a result, the cook loses his job. The goblin, though, has a going-away present for the cook: a special box. "Whatever you desire," the goblin explains, "name your wish, and knock on the lid of the box with your fingernail."[50] The box works just as the goblin promises, and like the shoemaking couple, the grateful cook lives contentedly for the rest of his life.

Getting Help

The goblins in these stories are eager to help others, but they give assistance only on their own terms. The cook does not ask the goblin for help, and neither do the shoemaker and his wife request assistance from the two goblins that eventually make the shoes. According to some tales, in fact, goblins will routinely refuse when they are asked for help. Even these reasonably kindhearted goblins have a contrary nature, and people who presume upon their friendship and compassion almost always fail to get the assistance they want.

The people that goblins choose to assist have two important characteristics. For one, they are never greedy. After getting the magic box from the goblin, for instance, the cook uses it sparingly. He asks it only for what he really needs. "A purse in my pocket," he

Described both as hobgoblin and fairy, the character of Puck in Shakespeare's A Midsummer Night's Dream *offers help to people without even being asked. A 1908 illustration depicts goblin tailors hard at work in a scene from the play.*

requests at one point, "with just a little money in it."[51] The shoe-maker and his wife, similarly, know that the shoes produced by the goblins are of exquisite quality. They could make enormous amounts of money by forcing the goblins to work for them. But they have no interest in doing so, and it bothers them not at all when the goblins leave after getting their clothes.

Second, the people helped by the goblins are almost always blessed by good fortune in the future, even long after the goblin is no longer present. That is true of the cook in "The Cook and the House Goblin." It is also true of Puck, a character in William Shakespeare's play *A Midsummer Night's Dream*. A small and saucy being, Puck is variously described as a hobgoblin and as a fairy. Along with play-ing jokes on unsuspecting farmers and travelers, Puck is known for giving help to people—unexpected, unrequested help much like the assistance the goblins offer the shoemaker. If those who get the as-sistance are properly grateful, Puck also brings them good fortune that may continue for years. "Those that Hobgoblin call you, and sweet Puck," says one of the fairies in the play, "you do their work, and they shall have good luck."[52]

A person who gets help from a goblin is expected to offer the goblin a gift in exchange. Indeed, giving gifts is the quickest way to a goblin's heart. In a Danish folktale called "The Goblin, the Student, and the Grocer," a grocer sets out treats each Christmas for the goblin that lives in his store. By doing so, he earns the goblin's complete loyalty. That is not a surprise: "As everyone knows," reads one retelling of the story, "if you give a goblin the things he likes most he will always be your friend."[53]

Gifts to helpful goblins must not be offered directly, though. Pre-senting a gift to a goblin in person, no matter how helpful or friendly that goblin has been, is a move certain to backfire. These goblins are

> ## Did You Know?
> Charles E. Carryl's 1884 children's book *Davy and the Goblin* is about a hob-goblin who takes a boy on a journey to introduce him to the world of (mostly be-nevolent) monsters.

often skittish by nature, and many of them prefer to work more or less anonymously. Certainly they would rather not be publicly acknowledged. In the Grimm Brothers' tale, the shoemaker and his wife handle their situation perfectly. Rather than risk embarrassing or frightening away the goblins by offering the new clothes in person, they simply leave the garments in plain sight. That is sufficient—and in fact, the only way to present the clothes without incident.

The World of Goblins

Of all the peculiar creatures said to inhabit the universe, from space aliens to dragons, few are as intriguing as goblins. The world of goblins includes creatures ranging in size from the almost microscopic Hinky Pink of Italian folklore to the cow-sized goblin of the Japanese tale "The Boy Who Drew Cats." It includes creatures that are determined to kill as many humans as they can, and beings that willingly help those same humans to complete what seem to be impossible projects. It encompasses tricksters that love to turn fresh milk sour, and thieves that steal teeth, gold, and any other object that strikes their fancy. Few legendary folk can boast half as many varieties, motivations, and forms as the goblin.

Nor do stories of goblins show any sign of disappearing soon. Tales such as *The Hobbit* and the *Elves and the Shoemaker* seem as popular as ever, and they are joined every year by new works produced by current writers and artists. Series such as the Spiderwick books, stand-alone novels like Tony Abbott's book *Kringle*, modern picture books that retell traditional goblin tales—all are part of the multitudes of goblin lore available today. Whether because of their helpfulness, their bloodthirstiness, or their interest in making mischief—or indeed, the combination of all three—goblins seem likely to be an important topic in literature and the arts for many years to come.

Source Notes

Introduction: Goblins in Legends and Literature

1. Quoted in Ian Donnachie and Carmen Lavin, *From Enlightenment to Romanticism, Anthology II*. Manchester, UK: Manchester University Press, 2004, p. 254.

Chapter One: A Field Guide to Goblins

2. J.R.R. Tolkien, *The Fellowship of the Ring*. New York: Houghton Mifflin, 1954, p. 317.
3. J.R.R. Tolkien, *The Hobbit*. Boston: Houghton Mifflin, 1966, p. 70.
4. Ruth Manning-Sanders, *A Book of Ghosts and Goblins*. London: Methuen, 1968, p. 14.
5. J.T. Petty, *Clemency Pogue: The Hobgoblin Proxy*. New York: Simon and Schuster, 2006, p. 23.
6. Manning-Sanders, *A Book of Ghosts and Goblins*, p. 90.
7. Molly Bang, *"The Goblins Giggle" and Other Stories*. New York: Scribners, 1973, p. 54.
8. George MacDonald, *The Princess and the Goblin*. New York: Knopf, 1993, p. 62; orig. pub. by Strahan & Co. in 1871.
9. Bang, *"The Goblins Giggle" and Other Stories*, p. 4.
10. Petty, *Clemency Pogue: The Hobgoblin Proxy*, pp. 70–72.
11. Tony Abbott, *Kringle*. New York: Scholastic, 2005, p. 13.
12. Barry Yourgrau, *Nastybook*. New York: HarperCollins, 2005, p. 182.
13. Tolkien, *The Hobbit*, p. 73.
14. MacDonald, *The Princess and the Goblin*, p. 67.
15. John Matthews, ed., *The Barefoot Book of Giants, Ghosts, and Goblins*. New York: Barefoot Books, 1999, p. 75.
16. MacDonald, *The Princess and the Goblin*, p. 146.
17. Tolkien, *The Hobbit*, p. 72.

18. William E. Griffis, "The Goblins Turned to Stone," in *Dutch Fairy Tales*, Baldwin Project, p. 169. www.mainlesson.com.

19. Tolkien, *The Hobbit*, p. 73.

20. Bang, *"The Goblins Giggle" and Other Stories*, p. 6.

21. Tolkien, *The Hobbit*, p. 72.

22. Ballads of Robin Goodfellow, "The Mad Merry Pranks of Robin Goodfellow," Robin Hood—Bold Outlaw of Barnsdale and Sherwood. www.boldoutlaw.com.

23. Abbott, *Kringle*, p. 15.

Chapter Two: Killers, Kidnappers, and Orcs: Goblins of Malice

24. Margaret Hodges, *The Boy Who Drew Cats*. New York: Holiday House, 2002.

25. Lafcadio Hearn, *Japanese Fairy Tales*. New York: Boni and Liveright, 1918, p. 35.

26. Tolkien, *The Hobbit*, p. 75.

27. Tolkien, *The Hobbit*, p. 116.

28. Manning-Sanders, *A Book of Ghosts and Goblins*, p. 15.

29. MacDonald, *The Princess and the Goblin*, p. 206.

30. Abbott, *Kringle*, p. 143.

31. Leonard Baskin, *Imps, Demons, Hobgoblins, Witches, Fairies, and Elves*. New York: Pantheon, 1984.

32. Petty, *Clemency Pogue: The Hobgoblin Proxy*, p. 90.

33. Maurice Sendak, *Outside over There*. New York: HarperCollins, 1981.

Chapter Three: Pranksters, Thieves, and Pinchers: Goblins of Mischief

34. Brian Froud and Terry Jones, *The Goblin Companion*. Atlanta: Turner, 1996, p. 76.

35. Tony DiTerlizzi and Holly Black, *Arthur Spiderwick's Field Guide to the Fantastical World Around You*. New York: Simon and Schuster, 2005, p. 84.

36. Ballads of Robin Goodfellow, "The Mad Merry Pranks of Robin Goodfellow."

37. Bang, *"The Goblins Giggle" and Other Stories*, p. 11.

38. Bang, *"The Goblins Giggle" and Other Stories*, p. 11.

39. Kate Greenaway, *Under the Window*. New York: McLaughlin, 1880, p. 45.

40. Manning-Sanders, *A Book of Ghosts and Goblins*, p. 92.

41. Manning-Sanders, *A Book of Ghosts and Goblins*, p. 30.

42. Megan McDonald, *The Hinky Pink*. New York: Atheneum, 2008.

43. Greenaway, *Under the Window*, p. 45.

Chapter Four: Fools, Victims, and Helpers: Good Neighbor Goblins

44. Enid Blyton, *The Enid Blyton Holiday Book*. London: Marston, p. 115.

45. Blyton, *The Enid Blyton Holiday Book*, p. 118.

46. Hans Christian Andersen, "The Goblin and the Woman," Research—Fairy Tales—Life & Works. www.andersen.sdu.dk.

47. Manning-Sanders, *A Book of Ghosts and Goblins*, p. 79.

48. Petty, *Clemency Pogue: The Hobgoblin Proxy*, p. 23.

49. DiTerlizzi and Black, *Arthur Spiderwick's Field Guide*, p. 85.

50. Manning-Sanders, *A Book of Ghosts and Goblins*, p. 35.

51. Manning-Sanders, *A Book of Ghosts and Goblins*, p. 35.

52. William Shakespeare, *A Midsummer Night's Dream*, in Burton Raffel, ed., *The Annotated Shakespeare*. New Haven, CT: Yale University Press, 2005, p. 30.

53. Matthews, *The Barefoot Book of Giants, Ghosts, and Goblins*, p. 50.

For Further Exploration

Books

D.L. Ashliman, *Fairy Lore: A Handbook*. Santa Barbara, CA: ABC-CLIO, 2006.

Ari Berk and Brian Froud, *Goblins!* New York: Harry N. Abrams, 2004.

David Colbert, *The Magical Worlds of Harry Potter*. New York: Penguin, 2008.

Tony DiTerlizzi and Holly Black, *Arthur Spiderwick's Field Guide to the Fantastical World Around You*. New York: Simon and Schuster, 2005.

Pierre Dubois, *The Complete Encyclopedia of Elves, Goblins, and Other Little Creatures*. New York: Abbeville, 2004.

Cassandra Eason, *A Complete Guide to Faeries and Magical Beings*. York Beach, ME: Redwheel/Weiser, 2002.

Jim C. Hines, *Goblin Hero*. New York: Daw, 2005.

George MacDonald, *The Princess and the Goblin*. New York: HarperFestival, 2004.

Web Sites

Andrew Lang's Fairy Books (www.mythfolklore.net/andrewlang). Andrew Lang was a collector and reteller of fairy tales, many of which are about goblins. This site archives his books of fairy tales.

Fairies World: Mythical and Folklore Names (www.fairiesworld.com/myths-mythology/folklore-names.shtml). A primer on names for various monsters, including some that are often applied to goblins.

Fantastic Fiction (www.fantasticfiction.co.uk). Information on writers of the supernatural and the books they wrote. Includes information about many people whose work involved goblins.

The Goblin Spider (www.baxleystamps.com/litho/hasegawa/hearn_5v_spider.shtml). The text and illustrations for a book about a Japanese goblin. Includes links to other books of Japanese folklore, some of which deal with goblins as well.

Pathfinder Roleplaying Game: "Goblin" (http://paizo.com/path finderRPG/prd/monsters/goblin.html). One of many information sheets about goblins and their powers as they appear in role-playing games.

Index

Picture Credits

About the Author

Stephen Currie lives in New York State with his family. He has written books and educational materials on subjects ranging from birthdays to baseball and from ecosystems to earthquakes. He has also taught students at various grade levels from kindergarten through college.